Five Deadly
Sins CEOs
Make in Sales

Five Deadly Sins CEOs Make in Sales

Jim Lewis

Five Deadly Sins CEOs Make in Sales

Copyright © 2009 Jim Lewis. All rights reserved. No part of this book may be reproduced or retransmitted in any form or by any means without the written permission of the publisher.

Published by Wheatmark®
610 East Delano Street, Suite 104, Tucson, Arizona 85705 U.S.A.
www.wheatmark.com

ISBN: 978-1-60494-228-6
LCCN: 2008942515

"Just Do It" is a registered trademark of Nike.

Blackberry® is a trademark of Research in Motion Ltd.

Except for real people who are Neil Rackham, Mike Bosworth, Geoffrey Moore, and Michael Jordan, all characters are fictional and are not intended to bear resemblance to real people. Any likeness is purely coincidental.

Contents

Introduction 1

1. Missed Expectations 5

2. The Board of Directors Meeting 13

3. Sin 1 — Confusing Marketing with Selling 23

4. Sin 2 — Failing to Understand How Buyers Buy 43

5. Sin 3 — Lacking a Repeatable, Auditable Sales Process .. 67

6. Sin 4 — Relying on Technology to Forecast Revenue 83

7. Sin 5 — Promoting Star Athletes to Head Coach 93

8. A New Direction 107

Appendix:
Jack's Meeting Notes 111
References 113

About the Author 115

Introduction

Forgive me, for I have sinned.

Not in the way this phrase is usually meant, but rather because I made business decisions and behaved in ways toward customers and prospects that didn't help me or my company. As the business leader of my company, I fell short. As CEO, I committed five deadly sins with respect to selling.

What did I do?

1. I was marketing, not listening to customers.
2. I failed to learn and understand how people buy.
3. I had no repeatable, auditable sales process.
4. I tried to use technology to solve a selling problem.
5. I promoted the best salespeople to management.

You might be thinking these errors are easy to fix. You may even think the last one, about promoting the best salespeople, is not even a problem. That's okay for now, but I do hope to show you some ideas to consider when making sales management hires and promotions.

And I warn you, these sins are not easy to fix because they are not easy to identify.

One reason that they are not easy to identify is because they don't neatly fit into a single context of management. For example, I haven't been able to find help on how to use technology in a sales process. In fact, there doesn't seem to be any books on the subject, and there are no management courses at the universities, as far as I am aware. I am still amazed how little, if anything, about the nuts and bolts of selling and sales management are offered at our prestigious MBA schools.

Second, these sins cut across management disciplines. Where can you find a book on the psychology of buyer behavior or on direct sales management that also discusses business processes and application technology? Quite simply, I don't think it exists!

As you look through the list, you may feel that you have been able to avoid one or more of the deadly sins. That's good. Your job will be easier because you can focus on the others. However, don't be fooled. All five concepts are interconnected, and as you will see from what happens to our fictional CEO character, they tend to pile on top of each other.

Introduction

Cracking the code, so to speak, requires making a lot of mistakes. Beyond just fixing businesses and improving results, it is useful to find out *how* and *why* things work, not just that they do work. This requires a degree of self-discovery, along with a lot of help from many other people—mostly very patient and understanding customers.

It's time to get started because you don't have much time. As a matter of fact, you have no time at all!

That is why this book is short.

If acknowledgement of a problem is the first step toward fixing it, then I hope this book can help you quickly get to the root causes. If you need help, ask.

Good luck.

ONE

Missed Expectations

As JACK RESSLER walked down the hall to the boardroom, he knew it was going to be a difficult meeting. The board of directors was assembled for their quarterly meeting and he would have to start by reviewing the draft of the next day's press release he held in his hand.

> *New York — Today, the Acme Company reported revenue flat from the prior year, missing analysts' projections. Jack Ressler, CEO, commented that, "although the pipeline was healthy and has grown by 12 percent over the prior year, several large prospective customers didn't close as forecasted...."*

What he couldn't understand was how three weeks ago the quarter had looked so promising. The first three quarters were flat, but he was expecting all the effort they had put into both sales and marketing to begin to pay off. At the start of the quarter, their pipeline of new business was the highest it had ever been, and he had enthusiastically shared this information with the board. He even brought screen shots of the "dashboard" that he could see from the computer on his desk.

At the beginning of the year, the company implemented a sales force tracking software application that allowed Jack instant access to a roll-up of all the deals that the sales team was working on. By clicking a few tabs on the screen, he could see the probability of close for each opportunity. It wasn't easy to get the salespeople to fill in the information. Mostly, they saw it as an invasion of their privacy and didn't see how it was going to help them sell.

Over time, however, they agreed to provide the information, which he could now see. Having a gauge on his desktop that showed a growing or shrinking pipeline and another that showed revenue to date gave him great comfort. Now if something started to slip, he could take action to fix it. Before, he felt like he was driving by looking at the rearview mirror: always looking at historical data to see ahead. His CFO, Sam Pelton, wasn't as convinced that the dashboard was useful. In Sam's opinion, the forecasts he regularly received from sales were rarely accurate. Still, Jack viewed any kind of data as better than none.

What happened to those critically important customer opportunities that were forecasted to close for months? There was intense focus on those deals during the preceding weeks. Jack's best people were working on them. Bill Smith, the vice president of sales, had personally visited each potential customer in the weeks prior and had been assured by the primary contact at each account that Acme was in the top spot and serious consideration was being given to the final proposal.

Jack distinctly remembered the phone conversation from the week before with Bill and the account reps as they crisscrossed the country to close business.

"Bill, you know how important it is that these contracts close by the end of the month. Can you give me an update on the current status?" asked Jack.

"Yes, Jack," replied Bill. Bill thought carefully about what he would say next.

Bill knew that everything, including quite possibly his career at the company, was riding on the outcome of this quarter. And as far as he knew, he was doing everything he could to bring in the business. He had instructed his account reps to stay close to their contacts in the accounts. He had them call frequently all quarter, with the idea of keeping the Acme name in the forefront of the prospects' minds. Bill had also offered an extra closing bonus incentive to keep the team motivated.

Closing new business was getting increasingly more difficult as some prospects and customers were not returning phone calls. That just made Bill all the more anxious, to the point that he started making the calls himself.

"As you know," began Bill, "competition has been heating up for quite some time, and people think our pricing is still pretty high. We've told our prospects that Acme is the best long-term provider, and we showed them numerous ROI analyses to prove our point."

Bill continued, "In the case of the Martin Company, you met with senior management and presented our strategic vision. That was well received according to the feedback we received later. So based on that, I think we have a good chance of winning that business."

Jack recalled flying out to Minneapolis a month before

to meet with the Martin Company managers. As part of his growth initiative plan, getting closer to customers was a top priority. That meeting was one of dozens in which he and his senior managers had participated. They felt that if they could get their story out to their key audience, public perception would change for the better. In his presentation, Jack shared how the company had grown from a small local firm to one with a national and international presence. With a famous private investment firm backing the company, he was certain Acme had the story, the financial resources, and the people to execute their strategy.

At the time, he thought the meeting went fairly well, but upon reflection, he couldn't quite decide why he felt that way.

"As for the rest," Bill concluded, "I have all the reps keeping close to their contacts. As soon as I hear something, you will be the next to know, and we know that—"

"Is there anything we should do on pricing to help them along?" interrupted Jack. "Would it help if you gave them an extra 2 percent for closing by the end of the month?"

Feeling desperate, Bill said, "Sure, we can try that, but I want to be careful not to derail their current deliberations."

"Okay, thank you, Bill. If you need anything else from me or the rest of the company, let me know."

Bill was an old dog professional salesman and was viewed by everyone who met him as likable and hard working. That was certainly the impression that Jack had when the two first met a year before. Bill was a divisional sales director at one of their competitors and had a track record of success throughout his career, earning the top performance award for the past five years. Because Bill's company was much smaller that really meant Bill was the top salesperson in the company.

It was no easy task convincing Bill to join Acme. The board of directors helped by granting additional stock options. At the time, Jack was ecstatic about the hire and felt that his first major decision would be to help improve the ailing company he had inherited. Increasing revenue was the number one goal, and having a top-flight sales executive would start them down that path.

As Jack walked into the boardroom, the knot in his stomach tightened. He wished that he had more answers. *Did we lose or is this just a delay? Did we get outsold? Were our prices too high?*

The next day, the company would have to announce they had missed their financial projections for the first time. If ever there was a stressful time since Jack was named CEO just over a year before, this was it.

His greatest fear and frustration were being realized.

TWO

The Board of Directors Meeting

HARRY GREEN SAT quietly as Jack presented the final slide. The fact that Harry had not asked more than a few questions during the entire two-hour meeting was unusual and disquieting. Normally the 6-foot 4-inch chairman was jumping out of his chair with enthusiasm. But that was not the case today.

Harry had started the company three years prior after convincing a few of his former investors to back him—again. This was the third in a string of start-ups that Harry had championed over the past ten years, each one more successful than the last. All the businesses had offered a mix of products and services, and Harry had a knack for being in the right place at the right time.

He was also known for being decisive and competitive, a trait he instilled in his management team. His style had been imprinted on the other companies he founded, as they were known for their aggressive selling tactics and flashy marketing gimmicks.

However, this time was different. As the buying spree of the the past ten years cooled off, it was becoming increasingly more difficult to simply announce a business, place ads in the trade magazine, hire a sales force, and then sit back and count the money. Competition was fierce, and buyers took longer to make decisions.

This time was also different because the investors had convinced Harry, now in his sixties, to hire a professional management team right from the start. Not only did they want to protect their investment, but they felt that the business could grow more rapidly if they had the right team in place at the beginning. Since the investors were willing to fund it, Harry didn't argue.

To that end, they hired one of the foremost executive recruiting firms in the country and tasked them with finding a CEO. It wasn't easy. Each of the board members had a different view as to the style, skills, and experience that were needed. A few of the board members wanted someone with a strong track record in operations and finance. Others wanted someone with a background in marketing. Harry wanted someone from sales.

Finding someone who met all of the criteria perfectly would be a near impossibility. Nevertheless, after several months of screening and interviews, Harry had a short list of three candidates, and after another few weeks of interviews and discussions, he had offered Jack Ressler the job.

Jack Ressler was the vice president of marketing at a small technology services company. He had been at that company for only a year when he received the call from the Acme headhunter. Normally, he would have passed on the opportunity. However, his current company was struggling and he had been frustrated with some of the decisions that the company had made. Still, he had been asked by the CEO to take on more responsibility to fix the problems, which included setting the strategic direction and overseeing product management and sales.

Jack's first job had been in sales working for a small computer company. After a few years of pounding the streets of New York selling financial planning using a PC, he started a software company. At twenty-five, Jack was head of a national sales team. He spent five years in the international division before the company was sold. Then he worked in a series of start-up companies, all of which were gobbled up by competitors. He considered it all a great experience. The business environment was always changing, so he had to adjust his plan and tactics constantly. Working the international side gave him full profit and loss (P&L) responsibilities for hundreds of millions of dollars. International experience provided a vast array of business challenges, not the least of which was negotiating in scores of different cultures.

He felt he was ready for his first CEO position, so he took the recruiter up on his offer to meet the company and its chairman, Harry Green.

Becoming the CEO of a company was nothing like what he thought it would be. During his whole career he had watched as other CEOs made both good and bad decisions. Most importantly, he thought that when he became CEO he would make better decisions. The day that he received word that he got the job was the high point in his professional career. Today was the low point.

Jack looked down the long expanse of the polished cherry conference table into the eyes of Harry Green.

The Board of Directors Meeting

He felt like a little boy who had let his father down. Jack was fond of Harry and had appreciated how he had taken him under his wing and provided morale as well as practical support. Harry had been his greatest supporter with the other board members as well. Jack could hear his heart pounding as silence hung over the room.

Harry rose to address the group and stretched his legs as a way of preamble.

"Jack, thank you for updating us on the business. At this time, I'd like to ask the management team to excuse themselves, except Jack," requested Harry. As was normally the case, each of the key senior executives attended some or all of the board meetings. This included the CFO, the VPs of sales and marketing, along with the COO. When the door had closed behind them, Harry addressed the board.

"Jack, please have a seat," said Harry. "It's clear to everyone that the results are not what we desire. Frankly, I am as perplexed as you are. We know about the numerous initiatives that you have undertaken in all parts of our business. Yet, there seems to be a problem with our ability to find new customers.

"In the old days, we could easily make up in activity what we lacked in finesse. And you know my adage of closing early and often has served me well. But the world has changed. Buyers are going to buying school. The Internet provides information to buyers that they use to establish buying criteria before we even have a chance to meet them. They use online auctions to have vendors bid for their business without consideration of our unique capabilities. Competition isn't just from companies in North America. It's coming from everywhere: China, India, South America, and Europe. We need a fresh look.

"After reviewing our current operations and after listening to your report, I feel that our ability to deliver great products and great service is unparalleled. We have a lot of talented and dedicated people. Furthermore, our finances and accounting operations are running fine. Finally, product management and engineering are also in good shape. In all these cases we have processes in place to plan, strategize, and execute our plans. Unfortunately, I don't feel that way about how we manage sales.

"We need to rethink how we find, nurture, and grow our relationships with customers. We need to have a systematic approach that gives us greater visibility, more predictability, and better results.

"It would be easy for us to place all the blame at your doorstep. As CEO, you are accountable for the results. However, as I discussed the issue with the outside directors, we came to the conclusion that a change in leadership would not solve the problem. In fact, we don't think it's necessary because we know what the problem is.

"Although you have managed most of the fundamentals of our business well, you have committed five deadly sins with respect to managing sales.

"For that reason, I have asked each of the board members to meet with you to discuss his or her perceptions of the problem and to make recommendations on how to address them. Each member will address one of the sins based on his or her own experiences and observations.

"Six days from now, we will meet again to review the situation and to chart a new course. Are there any questions?"

"No. Thank you for your support," replied Jack.

"Well then, meeting adjourned," concluded Harry.

With that, Harry and the other board members left the room.

Jack sat at the end of the conference table for a long time, mostly just to let his heart rate return to normal. His brain was working so fast he thought it might explode. He still heard the dull thumping of his heart, so he knew that it was still working.

What just happened, and what are the five deadly sins that Harry mentioned? he thought to himself.

Why had he not heard of them before?

In the past ten minutes, Jack had ridden a roller coaster of emotions from frustration and embarrassment to panic and, now, curiosity.

He looked forward to meeting with the board members. Although some had big egos, their business successes gave them certain bragging rights. And their experiences were far reaching. For Jack, humility began to set in.

In the morning, he would have his assistant, Sally, reschedule his week so he could meet with each of the

The Board of Directors Meeting

five board members. He would have to cancel his trip to Chicago, and he would have to push off meetings with his executive team until he understood what he should be doing.

At that moment, he did not know what to do next. So he just sat and pondered.

THREE

Sin 1— Confusing Marketing with Selling

IF FEAR HAD consumed Jack's thoughts in the days leading up to the board meeting, curiosity had consumed him ever since. The Monday following the meeting, Jack was deep in thought, wondering what his future would be. In particular, he thought about what the next few hours would be like.

Rather than looking for a new job, as he had thought would be the case, he was eagerly looking forward to meeting with the first board member, Paul Smith. It was Harry Green that had suggested Jack have these meetings, after what had been a rather unpleasant quarter-end board meeting the previous Friday. It was an odd response from Harry, who Jack fully expected to fire him. He wasn't sure, but he thought there was a glimmer of empathy and recognition in his face as Harry proposed this course of action.

Jack pulled his car into one of the many open slots in the parking lot of the local coffee shop. Paul suggested they meet there instead of the office, where peering eyes and ears might disturb them. Jack was happy with the idea because he wanted to have a quiet and relaxed setting. Since he did not know what to expect, he also wanted a way to gracefully escape if necessary.

"Good morning Jack," said Paul Smith as the two men met with a healthy handshake. "I found a table and chairs over there in the corner. Is that okay with you?"

Paul Smith was the most senior of the board members and had known Harry for over twenty-five years. He was the retired chairman and CEO of a large Fortune 500 manufacturing company that bore his family name. His company made everything from diapers to hand wipes. What really made Paul special was his understanding of marketing and sales.

"Yes, yes. That's fine," replied Jack.

"Good then. Let's get some coffee and get started.

"Jack, first I want to share with you that we think you are a highly capable and motivated CEO. There have been a great number of positive changes in the company since you took over, and I want to commend you for that. Some of those changes had a big impact, such as the changes in the engineering design process. Some were more subtle, like the way you added more capabilities to the service side of the business.

"In many companies, the role of the board is to monitor the activities of the company and to make sure that investors' interests are properly represented. However, in today's increasingly challenging marketplace and with Sarbanes-Oxley and other compliance and regulatory requirements, company boards must play a more participatory role in the operational side of the business. My colleagues and I were not planning to get too involved with sales, but when we all started to recognize patterns that we experienced ourselves, we decided to jump in."

Paul paused to take a sip of coffee and to let Jack respond.

"Paul, I very much appreciate the approach that you and the board are taking. I must admit that I was apprehensive about the whole idea since, as you said, most boards are hands off," offered Jack.

Over the weekend, Jack had recalled and reflected on his meteoric rise to CEO and the management decisions he had made along the way. What he realized in an important moment of humility was that once he had been promoted to CEO, he had abandoned the very thinking that was his source of success — asking for help. That included people inside the company as well as external resources who were experts in their fields.

He also came to realize that he was not taking full advantage of the skills and experience that were available to him. On the one hand, he felt that the CEO had to provide decisive leadership and direction. That was certainly an image he wanted to project. On the other hand, that same behavior could lead to a feeling of omnipotence. *Once you start believing all the hype and spin that you put out,* he thought, *things can go downhill pretty fast.*

"How do you feel about things today?" asked Paul.

"Uncertain, but I'm open-minded," replied Jack.

"Good," said Paul. "Let's continue. What was the last major purchase you made at a store, Jack?"

Sin 1—Confusing Marketing with Selling

Jack had to think for a few seconds before answering, "We just upgraded our TV in the bedroom to LCD/HD."

"When you went into that electronics store, did a salesperson approach you?"

"Yes."

"What did he or she say, and how did you respond?"

"Well, I started looking around and a young kid about twenty-five came up and asked me if I needed any help. I told him no, I was just going to look around."

Paul asked, "Did you need his help?"

"No. At least not initially," Jack replied.

"And why was that?"

"I already had a pretty good idea of what I wanted and of my approximate budget. I also looked online a few days prior and searched for brands, features, and other information about all the specifications and jargon."

"What if that same salesperson started telling you about the history of the company, its people, its financial status, its beliefs, and its approach toward customer service?" Paul asked.

"I'd think he was trying to sell me something, and I probably wouldn't trust him," said Jack.

"That's right. So why should the prospects that you are trying to reach feel differently if the same approach was used on them?"

"What do you mean?" Asked Jack

"Remember that trip to Minneapolis that you told the board about on Friday?"

"Yes"

"Tell me what happened. Describe the meeting agenda."

Jack began, "We went in to present our strategic direction and to initiate a dialogue around long-range issues that we could tackle together. We met in their board room and made the presentation there. I spoke for the first twenty minutes, and then my team took over. I thought it went well."

"Did it?" asked Paul.

Sin 1—Confusing Marketing with Selling

"They certainly seemed enthusiastic at the time, but I think you are trying to tell me something."

Ever since they left that meeting and had flown back home, Jack had been asking that very same question: was it a good meeting or not?

"Let me show you something," said Paul. "I clipped this off one of our competitors' website.

> *We believe that working with our customers as strategic partners allows us to demonstrate the greatness of our people and their ability to maximize the value of their contribution to our customers' success.*

"Now let me show you the Acme company overview statement.

> *Since our inception, we have been guided by core values that define our company and its people. We strive to help customers achieve global success and to avoid unnecessary risks.*

"Did you happen to have a slide in your presentation that included this statement, and was it discussed?" asked Paul.

"As a matter of fact, we did. I also mentioned that we

were ready and committed to help them in any way we could." At the time, Jack thought that this was their finest moment in the presentation and certainly the one he felt most passionate about.

Reading the two statements again left Jack with an uneasy feeling. He was beginning to see that his presentation materials, although useful in helping investors and the public at large know who they are, didn't do anything to help potential customers understand the specifics of how Acme could help them. The presentation was more of a positioning statement. And since they had done most of the talking, they hadn't let their prospective customer spend much time describing the critical business issues that they faced.

"Jack," began Paul, "how effective was the presentation at uncovering the underlying business needs of this prospect, and what were you trying to accomplish?"

"I am beginning to see your point. We were pitching them rather than taking time to diagnose and really understand their key issues.

"But, Paul," Jack continued, "how do we convince them that we really are a better company, particularly

Sin 1—Confusing Marketing with Selling

when the marketplace sees very little differentiation between what we offer and what our competitors offer? We thought that if I invested time in meeting them and told them about our approach and the resources and skills we have that we would have a jump start on the competition by setting the bar high."

Paul sat silent for a moment, deciding how to best get his point across.

"Let me tell you about an experience I had that could shed light on the subject," said Paul. "I recently added a garage addition to my house. Although it overran the budget and took twice as long to complete, it's now finished.

"One of the critical tasks in building the garage was the electric rough-in. In this step, all the wires are run through the walls, and the lights, outlets, and switch boxes are installed. I decided to interview electrical subcontractors from listings I found in the local yellow pages. I called three companies, and they all agreed to come to the house, review the plans, and tell me how much it would cost.

"The first company showed up a few days later, and the owner introduced himself. Mel was his name, and he arrived in a well-worn pickup truck. There were no markings on the truck, but it looked like it was stocked full of supplies. I showed Mel the electrical blueprints, and he proceeded to study them and walk around the project. We looked inside the car park area and then visited the second floor. During the whole time, he was looking up and down with a very inquisitive and studious look on his face. With his inspection finished, I asked him how much he thought it would cost. He said to be fair he would like to take a copy of the plan back to his office to study it further. He agreed to give me an estimate the next day.

"'Mel, can you tell me about your company?' I asked as the final question.

"He answered, 'A1 is a local company. We've been doing business in this town for thirty years, and I took over the business from my father. We have a couple guys, and since you're local, we'll give you a good price.'

"The next day, the second contractor showed up. He drove up in a brand new truck with the name Tri-State Electrical Contractors emblazoned on the side. A man jumped out of the truck and introduced himself as Pete. Pleasantries completed, we followed the same

Sin 1—Confusing Marketing with Selling

routine that I had with Mel. Pete was more inquisitive and wanted to know how long I had lived in the house, what my timeframe was for having the work performed, and who was doing the rest of the construction. I could not tell from his reaction whether the answers I gave him were helpful. In any case, I gave him a copy of the plan, and he said he would send me a written proposal within a week.

"Pete, can you tell me about your company?" I asked, wanting to be fair to each candidate.

"He answered, 'Tri-State Electrical Contractors is the largest contractor in the area. We have over two hundred employees and manage both residential and commercial projects. We're doing all the work for the new high school, and we also do work for the state. We can put our best team on this project and get it done quickly.'

"I thanked him for visiting. We shook hands, and he drove off. As he left, I stood in my driveway thinking that, based on the information so far, I could not decide which contractor to use.

"Was price going to be the determining factor? Is price the only issue? What sort of risk does each option present? Is bigger better? Is smaller better? Is someone with specialized residential experience better than someone with a broad range of unrelated skills? I just couldn't decide.

"Jack, which contractor would you chose?"

Jack replied, "I'm not sure either. Each has advantages. I guess it would depend on my prior experience with either a big or small company. I probably have a built-in bias."

"This is the dilemma that prospects and customers face all day, and we, as sellers, don't make the job any easier," continued Paul.

Paul looked at Jack to see his reaction. Jack was nodding his head in agreement so Paul continued.

"The following day, the third contractor, Tom from Tom's Electric, arrived. He had an average looking pickup truck without markings. I sucked in my breath and waited for the next round to start. Tom introduced himself and asked, 'How can I help you?'

"I gave Tom the blueprint to explain to him what I had

in mind. His first question was, 'What are you going to use the garage for?'

"I told him about my upstairs office, but I also mentioned that the downstairs area, in addition to housing my daughter's car, would serve as a wood shop and as storage for other yard equipment like my tractor.

"'Where do you do your woodworking now?' Tom asked me.

"In the other garage, I replied.

"'Can you show me?' he asked.

"I proceeded to open the door of the existing garage, and as the door slowly opened, I had the same sinking feeling I had as a kid when my mother opened my closet doors. There, stacked to the ceiling, was all the junk and shop equipment that eventually was going to be moved into the new space.

"Tom turned to me and asked, 'Until now, have you been using this existing garage space as a shop?'

"Yes," I replied.

"'I notice,' he continued, 'that there is only one outlet

in here, and it's a 15 amp ground fault circuit (GFI). Does that cause any problems when you try to run more than one piece of equipment at the same time: for example, running both your saw and that big shop vacuum?'

"Instantly, I knew he was on to something. Most garages in the United States have a single 15 Amp GFI in the garage. They are installed primarily for use with small appliances. Most wood shop equipment is power hungry and needs 20 amps or more. What Tom knew, or suspected, was that I was constantly tripping the circuit by overloading it. In fact, if you ever tried to run an extra refrigerator off this circuit and then try to vacuum your car, the circuit pops!

"Tom looked at me and said, 'Mr. Smith, you have only one circuit in the new garage space. Although it is a 20 amp circuit, you are likely to continue to have the same problem. Why don't we split the circuit in two and add a breaker so you have a total of 40 amps?'

"That's a great idea," I said.

"We then proceeded to look more closely at the other power needs of my upstairs office. Ultimately, we decided to add a few more circuits there as well.

Sin 1—Confusing Marketing with Selling

"While we were discussing these changes, Tom mentioned that although the additional lines would not be difficult to install it would require one more change. The circuit breaker box did not have enough openings to accommodate the extra lines. We would need to go to a twenty slot breaker box versus the ten slot breaker box that was in the plan.

"Again, I agreed with the change. And so it went.

"Jack, who do you think got the job?" asked Paul.

"I would have to say that Tom got the job, but wasn't he more expensive?" asked Jack.

"Tom was about 10 percent more expensive than the other two. But as a result of understanding my needs and the application, I had a significantly higher comfort level about the job being done right the first time. I also knew that if any unforeseen issues arose I could work with Tom and his team to sort out the details. In fact, I was confident that he could anticipate issues that I had not thought about. That would save me headaches later and, potentially, a lot of unnecessary costs."

Jack realized that at Acme they were thinking about their business in entirely the wrong way. Considering the story that Paul had just told, Jack was astonished at how simple and effective the whole experience was at moving Tom's company to the top of the list.

Jack knew that there were lots of other companies that had the same offerings as Acme. That makes it difficult for customers to differentiate, he recognized. It was the same challenge that the electrical contractors have with the wiring buried inside the walls of Paul's garage. Everyone uses the same wiring materials and has to follow strict national code compliance laws. All the work is inspected by a town official for safety. In other words, there is virtually no apparent product differentiation.

Jack concluded that the main point Paul was making was that, initially, it's not as important how much the prospect knows about you and your company, but how much the prospect feels you know about him or her.

Jack also commented to Paul that the positioning of the first two contractors did nothing to help him decide which to use. In fact, he realized that if he had been predisposed to go to either a big or small firm, the other would have been eliminated immediately.

By thinking about the way Paul would use the space

Sin 1—Confusing Marketing with Selling

and his electrical needs, Tom was able to ask probing and qualifying questions to help him see a better solution. He had effectively extended Paul's requirements beyond simply executing the blueprint plans, something akin to a request for proposal (RFP). The first two had just assumed that it was right because it was in writing.

It was this extra bit of insight and diagnosis that allowed Paul to convince himself that there was more value in the services that Tom could provide.

Paul sat back and looked Jack in the eyes.

"Marketing has a lot to do with defining who you are as a company, what position you want to take in the marketplace, and how you stack up against competitors.

"Selling, however, involves a very personal and intimate dialogue between a buyer and seller. It takes a lot of guts for a prospect to be willing to share their most secret details about problems that they can't solve themselves. If a buyer doesn't feel that you understand their issues and challenges, you are very unlikely to get much information from them. So if you start by talking about *you* instead of asking about them, you are not going to get very far in the relationship.

"Jack, remember the salesman in the electronics store? How much information did you initially share?" asked Paul.

"Not much," he replied. "Nothing in fact."

"So why should you expect any different behavior or reaction from others than what you feel yourself?" Paul challenged.

"I get it, I get it," said Jack. "In fact, I may have made the problem even worse by directing the salespeople to follow my lead. They're looking for me to help them position the company and our offerings as unique and different from our competitors by coming up with key words and phrases that we pitch. That I pitch. They are just copying me!

"Instead of taking the time and effort to understand the needs of potential customers and exploring ways we could help them, what you called an intimate dialog, our sales effort today is largely about positioning the company and pushing our messages."

Sin 1—Confusing Marketing with Selling

"Exactly," said Paul.

"So the first deadly sin is that I have confused marketing and selling," said Jack.

"Yes."

There was a long silence as the two men stared at each other. Jack realized that he had created part of the problem Acme faced today. *That's okay*, he said to himself. *If recognition of a problem means that you are partway to a solution, then there's hope.*

Jack extended his hand across the table—a gesture of both acknowledgment and gratitude.

He said, "Thank you, Paul; that was very helpful and humbling."

"You're welcome," replied Paul. "Do you feel you know how to solve the problem?"

"Not yet," Jack replied honestly. "I think I need to find out about the other sins first."

"Yes," said Paul again. "You will be meeting with Sara Lipmann tomorrow. She'll continue where we left off."

"I look forward to it," said Jack.

With that, Jack left the coffee shop and headed to the office.

FOUR

Sin 2—
Failing to Understand
How Buyers Buy

SARA LIPMANN WAS the CEO of Lipmann industries, a company her father had started nearly forty years earlier. A graduate of a small liberal arts college, Sara had decided not to work for her father when she graduated. Instead, she worked for several smaller companies in nonrelated industries and then went back to school to receive her MBA a few years later. Four years ago, at the urging of her father, Sara decided the time was right for her to join her father's company as CEO. The education and experience that she gained previously paled in comparison to the on-the-job training of running a large company. Her appointment included assuming the board of directors position at Acme that her father held.

What she was about to share with Jack Ressler was not

something she learned while getting her MBA or in any of the other companies she had worked for. She wished she had because it would have saved her a lot of grief.

Lipmann Industries was located just outside the more populated area where Jack lived, so it took little more than half an hour to make the trip. The day before, he had learned that his excessive enthusiasm to tell prospects and customers all about his company was not the best way to initiate a selling opportunity. He also began to wonder about the effectiveness of the standardized sales presentation that the salespeople used. Both sales and marketing spent hours arguing and then refining the messaging, value propositions, and key points about Acme's competitive advantage. Marketing had insisted that in order to position the company properly and consistently everyone in sales should use the same presentation. He was beginning to question the logic of that decision and would have to revisit the issue later. Right now his thoughts were on the next few hours and his meeting with Sara Lipmann to find out about the second of the five deadly sins.

Jack was ushered into a meeting room that seemed to be prepared for anything. There were a half dozen easel pads scattered around the room with boxes of

Sin 2—Failing to Understand How Buyers Buy

markers placed strategically in each corner. Along the entire length of one side of the room was a single white expanse—the ultimate white board—and it was filled with a dazzling array of notes, graphs, and diagrams in a multitude of colors. Some of the notes stated in no uncertain terms DO NOT ERASE.

Sitting on the conference room table was a collection of telephone equipment with spiderlike attachments meant to support conference calls for at least twenty people. As Jack scanned the room, he noticed a sign above the white board that declared War Room. Below the sign, in smaller letters, read a quote from Winston Churchill: "Plans are worthless. Planning is everything."

As he was reading the quote, Sara Lipmann entered the room carrying a stack of books, and a yellow notepad.

"Good morning, Jack," said Sara as she held out her hand to greet Jack.

"Good morning, Sara" replied Jack. "I can't help but be amazed at your war room."

"We're not really at war, but the parallels to what happens on the battlefield are not dissimilar to our business environment. Everything changes constantly, so we felt that we needed a place where the executives and managers could meet to assess, strategize, and then develop a plan of execution as the world around us changes. One of my first challenges when I took over day-to-day operations from my father was to referee between the sales and marketing organizations. We started in this room one morning and worked well into the night. Overcome with exhaustion, we simply got up and left everything as it was. The next morning when we came back to the room, we just picked up where we left off. We then realized that our planning efforts should be continuous. Instead of having the cleaning people straighten things up at the end of the day, we just have them leave it, so in the morning, we can continue where we left off."

Sara asked Jack to be seated and then continued.

"As you will soon see, I have a mountain of information about selling and the sales process. This information was largely responsible for helping me to understand selling from the buyer's viewpoint. A viewpoint that, I admit, was not the way we used to look at the world here at Lipmann Industries."

Sin 2—Failing to Understand How Buyers Buy

"One of the first discoveries, or maybe I should say agreements, was that we did not have a workable definition of what selling is. As we went around the room, everyone had an opinion based on his or her personal experience of both selling and being sold to. In fact, there were more opinions than there were people in the room! Without some understanding of what selling is or should be, it became clear that neither our selling nor our marketing efforts were going to be very effective.

"We worked toward finding a definition of selling, but that didn't really help much. All the wording we came up with sounded nice, but it didn't answer some key questions:

- Why do we win, and why do we lose?
- How can we determine our chances of winning earlier in the sales cycle?
- When are buyers ready to buy?

"It came down to a lack of understanding of how buyers buy. We simply didn't know — or at least we could not codify the process so that everyone could evaluate a selling opportunity and reach, essentially, the same conclusion about our chance of success. If we don't know how buyers buy, how can we possibly improve our performance to create a better buyer experience? The answer was we couldn't.

"Finally, there are many people besides salespeople who interact with customers and prospects on a daily basis. If we were going to improve the customer's experience with our company, we would need a broad understanding across the company about what should be happening, when, and by whom. Instead, thousands of hours were spent by sales, marketing, engineering, support, and finance arguing about how each customer issue and opportunity should be handled. It was quite painful, aside from being inefficient."

Jack had faced many of these same issues early in his tenure at Acme and felt that the communication between the operating parts of the company had improved. Yet he also knew that the amount of time people spent in meetings discussing problems was still too much and that the phone lines between sales and the rest of the company were burning up with issues. All of that was taking people away from actually doing something to solve problems and help customers.

"Sara, how did you get to the bottom of this problem," asked Jack, genuinely interested.

Sin 2—Failing to Understand How Buyers Buy

"Our 'ah-ha' moment came when one of our sales executives shared information he learned during a sales training class at his former employer," replied Sara.

"Part of what I am going to share with you," began Sara, "I learned from the executive, and the rest is supplemented with information and research from several well-known authors. Most importantly, though, when we used this information as the basis of our approach to customers, it worked!"

As Sara began to speak, Jack realized that this was no ordinary chief executive. First, she was responsible for day-to-day operations of the business. Beyond that, she helped the sales organization facilitate communication, the delivery and processing of orders, contracting, and the scheduling of technical resources. She also helped with general administration so that salespeople could focus on customer calls. More importantly, she was focused on establishing a best practices approach to managing and executing their standardized sales process. To do that, Sara not only had to be able to demonstrate effective sales techniques, but also she had to have the ability to break down all the different steps, sales stages, and skills of the sales process so that other people could learn and then emulate them.

Sara began, "There are three factors that dramatically affect the selling process today:

- Buyer experience with bad selling;
- Buyers going to buying school
- The Internet

"When I first learned to sell, some of the more prominent selling approaches included closing early and closing often, to always be closing, learning how to overcome objections, and other manipulative techniques. I was also told that after I probed for a pain that I should quickly move to a proof stage, where I could demonstrate our products and services.

"The world has changed, and these techniques just don't work.

"In fact, twenty years ago the only way a prospective customer could learn about your company and its offerings was to speak to a salesperson. Today, almost every potential buyer will conduct some amount of research on the Internet before they contact your company. That means that the stage the buyer is in is much farther along in their deliberations than in the past. In turn, that presents some unique selling challenges. But

Sin 2—Failing to Understand How Buyers Buy

first, let's talk about some principles of buyer behavior.

"In the 1980s, Neil Rackham conducted research on selling behaviors and skills. The intent of the research was to uncover reasons why the top salespeople did better than others. At the time, many of the biggest U.S. corporations had rather rigorous sales training programs that were touted as the best in the world. Nevertheless, not wanting to be complacent, they sought empirical evidence of individual sales performance to further strengthen their process and training programs.

"Mr. Rackham conducted more than ten thousand observations of salespeople in real selling situations. In the end, he reached some rather unexpected conclusions. The research, much to the chagrin of senior management at those top companies, debunked the foundation of the traditional selling methods of probing, objection handling, and closing. All of this is well documented in his 1988 book, *SPIN Selling*.

"Arguably, his major contribution at the time was the recognition that buyers transit different buyer stages. However, the model was largely incomplete until a former Xerox executive, Michael Bosworth, pioneered the concept of a structured sales process. Despite their extensive sales training program, even Xerox was a victim of the 80-20 Rule: 80 percent of their revenue was produced by 20 percent of the salespeople.

"Bosworth's methodology turned the looking glass around to start with an understanding of how buyers buy rather than exclusively focusing on how sellers should sell.

"When I first heard this, I though it sounded very powerful. Consider this: A single buyer may buy different goods and services differently. Different buyers buy different goods and services differently. With so many combinations of buyer behaviors, it's hard to see how a single style of selling could adjust to these different circumstances."

"And why a single sales presentation or approach will miss the mark more often than it hits it," interrupted Jack.

"That's right," replied Sara. "I'd like to show you some examples of different buyer profiles. First, may I ask you a question?"

"Sure," replied Jack.

Sin 2—Failing to Understand How Buyers Buy

"When did you purchase your first Blackberry®?"

"About ten years ago. Why?" asked Jack.

"How long did it take you to decide that you wanted that device once you saw it?"

"I think it was a very quick decision. It may have been less than a minute."

"Based on that," said Sara, "Geoffrey Moore would describe your buying preference as an 'Innovator.'"

"Who is Geoffrey Moore?" asked Jack.

Sara reached into her pile of books and pulled out *Crossing the Chasm*.

"Mr. Moore was trying to find out why certain types of companies fall into a revenue chasm despite early success with new product offerings. In the course of his analysis, he discovered something related to marketing and strategy because it has a great deal to do with the way companies sell. More importantly, it had everything to do with the way buyers buy

"In your case as an innovator and as it relates to the purchase of your Blackberry®, your buyer characteristic suggests that you were likely intrigued by the technology for its own sake. Not only could you form a vision of how and why you would use the product, but you were also willing to take on all the risks associated with an un-market-tested product. Not everyone is so inclined. According to Moore there are five buyer types: Innovator, Early Adopter, Early Majority, Late Majority, and Laggard. Although Moore was describing the propensity of people and companies to buy technology, we have found that the same characteristics apply to any kind of purchase whether its high tech, low tech, or services."

Sara handed the book to Jack.

"We don't have time to go over all the facets of this model," continued Sara, "but I do want to give you a concrete example of how this can have an important impact on the way your company approaches the marketplace and how your salespeople sell."

Sara walked over to one of the paper easels and wrote down the five buyer types:

- Innovator
- Early Adopter
- Early Majority

Sin 2—Failing to Understand How Buyers Buy

- Late Majority
- Laggard

She began to relate an experience she had in her first selling job. She was told by her sales manager to take her sales kit of collateral and data sheets and to start calling on prospects. At the time, she was selling a new laser-powered measuring device. At each sales call, she would present the product and begin describing all its features. Early on, a high percentage of calls resulted in sales. After a while, she got better at watching the eyes of her prospects to detect interest. If the prospects eyes began to twinkle, she was pretty sure she would get an order. Alternately, if the prospect's eyes began to glaze over or if the person began to fidget, she would simply move on to the next call. At the time, she concluded that she must be off her game on those days or for those situations that she could not generate enthusiasm for her product. So she kept trying to spin the presentation differently to see what worked. The problem—and the frustration—was that there didn't seem to be a pattern. As she and others in her company pounded the streets, the time between sales became longer and longer.

What happened, as Sara discovered after reading Moore's book, is that she and the other salespeople in her company had picked all the low-hanging fruit. In other words, of the total market, only a small portion of the buyers—the Innovators and Early Adopters—could simply see a product and decide on their own that they wanted it and how they would use it.

Sara drew the following diagram on the board:

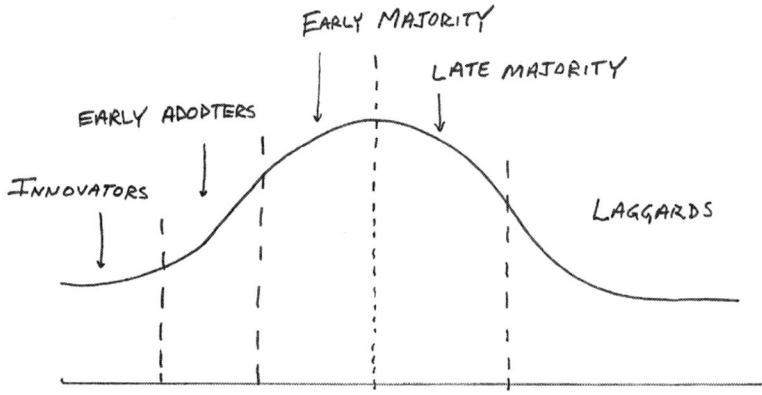

"as you can see, she explained to Jack, "Innovators and Early Adopters represent a relatively small portion of the total market as indicated by the height of the curve. Our selling approach was efficient when we were selling to these early buyers, but pretty soon we ran out of buyers."

"What about the Early and Late Majority buyers?" asked Jack. "They seem to be the largest category of buyer. Why not target them?"

Sin 2—Failing to Understand How Buyers Buy

"That is precisely what we did. However, there is a paradox," answered Sara. "The characteristic of an Early Majority buyer is quite different. They are much more cautious and pragmatic. They are not easily swayed by the opinions of people who are willing to take the kinds of risks that Innovators will. In fact, risk takers scare later-stage buyers. Instead, Early and Late Majority buyers want more evidence of the stability of the vendor, details of product warranties, service capabilities, financial strength, and so on. Innovators and Early Adopters are lousy references for this group of buyers. Therefore, the selling approach has to be different. What do you think the reaction was from Early Majority buyers when I attempted to use the same selling approach I had used to reach Innovators and Early Adopters?"

"Not good," acknowledged Jack. "I see your point. Not only are the reasons for the purchase different, but also the type of evidence needed to support that decision is vastly different."

"That's right. It gets worse. Think again about your own experience. What was the decision process and what was important to you when you purchased your last washing machine for your home? Was it spontaneous and all you had to do was look at the choices, like when you purchased your PDA, or were there other factors?"

"It was completely different. My wife and I discussed some general requirements before we began shopping, but I am sure that she checked out the reliability ratings, energy usage, and reputation of the various brands."

"So what that means is you behave like an Innovator when purchasing one type of item but like an Early Majority, Late Majority, or even Laggard when purchasing something else."

"Yes, I see. This is far more complex than I thought," said Jack.

"There is another factor that I should mention," responded Sara. "When your organization sells to another company, is there a sole buyer who is the decision maker or are there many people involved?"

"Usually, there are many people involved, including the decision maker. It depends on the situation, but we could have at least ten or more people involved," said Jack.

"What about all of the buying characteristics of those

Sin 2—Failing to Understand How Buyers Buy

people? Does your current selling approach take that into account?" inquired Sara.

Jack was silent. He stared at the notes on the easel and realized that his entire mental model of how sales should work was unraveling. It wasn't simply a matter of getting the pitch right, they had to figure out who they were talking to and what the buyer characteristics were before they even said a word. "Sara, I hope you have a way to help me convey this to my people," said Jack.

"Yes, I'll give you the name of someone who can help you. There is one more thing," said Sara, somewhat apologetically.

"I'm ready," said Jack, knowing that his perspective on selling was rapidly changing. Into what, he wasn't yet sure.

"Remember Michael Bosworth, the guy from Xerox who built on Rackham's work and developed a customer-centric approach to selling?" asked Sara rhetorically. "This is the diagram of shift buyer concern that he developed from Mr. Rackham's base research." Sara drew the folliwing graph on the white board.

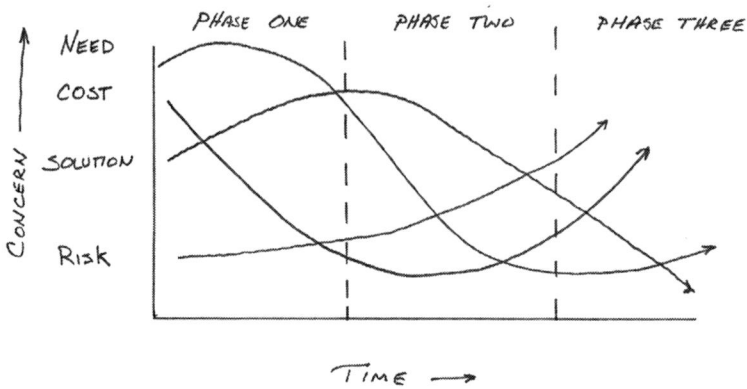

"Looks complicated," commented Jack.

"At first glance, I agree," Sara responded. "But once we applied this buyer model to our approach to customers, everything changed for the better.

"In simple terms, according to Bosworth, different factors called *concerns* have different levels of importance at different times during a typical buying process. Although everyone does not act exactly the same way all the time, this model is surprisingly accurate. By observing buyer behavior and the questions they ask, or the response to our questions, we can reasonably predict which stage a buyer is in. Let me give you an example.

Sin 2—Failing to Understand How Buyers Buy

"Let's say one of your salespeople receives a call from a potential customer, maybe as a result of seeing your name in a trade magazine. Here is how the call sounds:

> Hi, my name is Joe North, and I am a project leader at XYZ Company. We just got budget approval for a project we've wanted to pursue for some time, and we'll need some help. I've heard great things about your company and want to ask that you send some people over to give us a demo of your products and pricing information. Also, we are on a fast track and will need a proposal in two weeks.

"How would your sales organization respond to this?" asked Sara.

"I suppose they would attempt to further qualify the opportunity. I am sure they would accept the meeting invitation to meet the prospect," said Jack.

"Okay. And let's say the salespeople came back enthusiastic about the meeting. How would they likely grade the opportunity?"

"I would think they would rank it fairly high," said Jack. "The prospect has a budget, a time frame and they know what they want. That seems like a fast track opportunity."

"Before we better understood how buyers buy, Lipmann would have responded the same way," said Sara.

"But ...?" asked Jack

"What if I told you that Joe had already spent months with one of your competitors, ironing out the details of the products and services they would need to solve their business issue? Instead of being at the beginning of phase one, where you could influence the final specification, this buyer is at the end of phase one about to move to the beginning of phase two. How can we tell? Note the crossing of the NEEDS line with the SOLUTION line. This is the demarcation between the two stages. It's a pretty good bet that the prospect already knows what they want and from whom they want to buy. The only reasons to get your company involved would be to validate their decision or to set up a pricing shoot-out. Most companies require a three-vendor evaluation process even though the outcome is usually rigged."

"That makes sense, but how do we find that out in the middle of the sales process?" asked Jack.

Sin 2—Failing to Understand How Buyers Buy

"One way to smoke them out would be to start asking questions that would normally come at the beginning of phase one. Those questions would be about their current circumstances and why they need help from you. Buyers in early stages of research are often very willing to share this kind of information. Do you think Joe would be willing to have a long meeting to go back over theses subjects?"

"Probably not," replied Jack.

"So using the diagram as a map, we can surmise two things: First, you are not the lead vendor. Someone else was there first. Second, it's unlikely that your salespeople could uncover enough business justification or necessary understanding of the prospect's current environment to build a competitive position. Buyers generally do not want to go backward in the buying process.

"A second clue would be the request for pricing early in the discussions. As you will note from the diagram, pricing plays an important factor but is the least important during phase two. A potential buyer's heavy emphasis on price very early in discussions with your salespeople might be an indication they plan to use you to negotiate against their lead vendor. This is a very common buyer tactic.

"The whole point of the model is to demonstrate that buyers follow a fairly predictable process and that knowing which concerns are more important at each stage helps salespeople identify the buyer stage and avoid bad behavior. We spoke earlier about some of the older methodologies that promoted closing early and often. The fact of the matter is that proper alignment with the buyer during all three stages is critical to predictable and repeatable sales success. It is only toward the end of the process, when all other issues and concerns have been dealt with, that the buyer is finally in a position to make a decision to buy. When salespeople try to accelerate movement through the stages by using closing techniques, discounting, and other annoying tactics, the results are usually bad. Just as you can detect a telemarketing call when you answer the phone, buyers know when they are being sold to. Most don't like it, but they wont necessarily tell you.

"One final thing I should mention relates back to Moore's model of buying types. Despite their apparent differences, all of Moore's buyers transit the same buying stages. The primary variations are the speed at

Sin 2—Failing to Understand How Buyers Buy

which they pass through each stage and the amplitude of each concern."

Sara, finished with her presentation, sat down across from Jack.

The material that Sara shared was extremely powerful and eye opening for Jack. Up to this point, Jack really did not have a behavior model that adequately described how buyers buy. All his reference points about selling had been rooted in the capabilities of individual salespeople. Even his own selling experience was based on a trial and error approach interspersed with his charisma. He realized that there were thousands of selling decisions that he and others had made that were just guesses. Now he understood the second deadly sin: he and his company did not understand how buyers buy.

FIVE

Sin 3—
Lacking a Repeatable, Auditable Sales Process

FOR TWO DAYS Jack felt like he was drinking from a fire hose. He had met with two board members so far and realized that his education was just beginning. For years he had believed that selling was art, not science. It was becoming increasingly evident that there are recognizable patterns both in the way people make decisions about buying products and services and in the way successful salespeople align with those behaviors.

The next person on his list of board members to meet was George Purdum, the general manager of a mid-sized technology consulting company headquartered in the city. It would take Jack just over an hour to reach the office by train. While he was standing on the platform waiting for the express train, he took the opportunity to people watch. Trying not to be too obvious, he looked in the faces of those with him on the platform. Everyone seemed to be staring into space, facing forward and looking at nothing in particular. *How do all of those different people buy things?* He turned his head and looked lengthwise down the other direction of the platform. There were more people also looking forward into space—*more people and, potentially, many different buyer styles and behaviors. No wonder our sales results are so erratic.* He visualized a box with an assortment of keys. For each person on the platform there was a unique key that would unlock their buying type. *If that's the case, how can I possibly know if the key our salespeople choose will fit the lock?* For that matter, he knew that up to that point they had really only been using one key—essentially, one sales pitch.

Jack realized there was another problem with their approach, and that had to do with the way the salespeople and Bill Green, his vice president of sales, evaluated and estimated the probability of a win. The discussions he had with Bill about specific opportunities were like describing the mood of each person he saw on the station platform. Not only would it be difficult to uncover their mood during an initial meeting, it's likely that it would change during the days, weeks, and months to

Sin 3—Lacking a Repeatable, Auditable Sales Process

follow. He knew for sure that the whole approach was flawed, and relying on Bill to filter and interpret the input he received from his salespeople was imprecise at best.

Jack sat and thought about the challenges as the train rattled along the sixty-five minute trip into the city. When he emerged from the tracks, he was carried by the flow of other commuters down the long underground corridor and up the escalator into the bright sunlight. He grabbed a cab for the short ride uptown to the offices of LightStick Technologies and rode the elevator to the twenty-third floor. The receptionist was expecting him. She issued him a security pass and then escorted him down the hallway to wait in George's office.

It was 7:45 A.M., and the office was already buzzing with activity. After a few minutes, George returned to his office and greeted Jack warmly.

"Good morning. Any trouble finding us," asked George.

"Not at all. The directions were perfect."

"Good. I understand you have already met with Paul and Sara. How's it going so far?"

"Well, so far I've learned that I have a lot to learn. You know that we — I — put a lot of energy into getting Acme to be more efficient in designing and developing products and services, implementing extensive customer care programs, and systematizing and quantifying our progress. I realize that we may have put a nice wrapper around our sales effort, but the core engine needs to be redesigned."

"Do you have any questions about the three buyer stages or Moore's theory of buyer types that Sara showed you?" George asked.

"We covered the material rather quickly, so I want to go back and read the two books that Sara gave me. She also provided the name of the team who helped her. I'll have to call them for a follow-up next week."

Jack continued, "I recognized a few sales opportunities that we lost without having any idea at the time *why* we lost them. By comparing the model with our approach and behavior at the time, I can see that we assumed the prospect was squarely in our camp when they were not. We were being used to round out the

Sin 3—Lacking a Repeatable, Auditable Sales Process

field of competitors and were never really a contender. I didn't tell Sara this yesterday, but it certainly was an ah-ha moment for me. It was also a rather painful discovery."

"I see," said George. "That is excellent, because with the tools and understanding of how buyers buy, you and your team can begin to diagnose specific sales opportunities based on a common benchmark. You have to realize that while there is some science to this method, not all sales situations will be identical, and you will still have to rely on some judgment and experience to select the right tactics and strategies. But having a benchmark against which to compare different situations and a common sales process language will give you an enormous advantage."

"Yes, I am beginning to see that. I still have a question about the salespeople and their approach. At this point, I think we could agree on the buyer stages, but all the salespeople have different styles and tactics. How do we figure out what works and what doesn't work? For that matter, should they all do the same thing?"

"I am glad you asked. That's the subject of today's discussion."

"Great! Let's dig in."

"All right, Jack, have you attended any type of musical concert or performance recently," George asked.

"Yes, my wife Sally and I attended a concert at the university a few weeks ago. Our daughter was singing in the choir."

"How was it?"

"We enjoyed it very much." Jack almost launched into a full description of the event and how much he enjoyed watching and listening, but he stopped himself.

"Describe it to me," said George.

"What do you mean?"

"Tell me the details. What did you hear?"

Jack sat, puzzled. He could describe the ambiance; he could describe the concert hall; he could describe the décor—but he was not sure how to describe the music he heard.

"I'm not sure I can."

Sin 3—Lacking a Repeatable, Auditable Sales Process

"Precisely. Now think about a meeting between one of your salespeople and a prospect. After the meeting was over and your salesperson returned to the office, how did he or she describe the meeting? How meaningful are some of the details of the call report?"

"If they think the meeting went well, they report as much," Jack said.

"Okay," said George, "that's fine for now. Now let's think about the prospect. Let's say that immediately after he or she left the meeting with your representative, the prospect went straight to another meeting on a different topic. Thirty minutes into that second meeting, how many details from the first meeting do you think the prospect retained?"

"I suppose there would be a steep drop-off."

"Yes, also correct. So how would that prospect describe the meeting?"

"I suppose either good or bad."

"And what if that person's boss didn't ask about the meeting until the next day? How would your prospect summarize the key points that your salesperson sought to make?"

"I'm not sure. It would depend on the individual. That sounds pretty weak doesn't it?"

"Therein lies both the problem and the opportunity. After sales calls, most salespeople write a follow-up letter or email." George handed Jack a letter. "Usually, they start like this:

> *Dear John,*
>
> *It was a great pleasure to meet with you and your team yesterday. We are certainly looking forward to working with you to provide you the best products and services our company can provide.*
>
> *As we told you, Acme Company has received top marks in the industry for it's ...*

Jack read the letter and then handed it back to George.

"What do you think," asked George.

"Sounds fairly typical."

"Yes, it does. This letter has been poisoned by the opinion of the salesperson, and it does little to reaffirm that the salesperson understands the critical business is-

Sin 3—Lacking a Repeatable, Auditable Sales Process

sues the prospect faces and the capabilities that might be needed to address the problem. Now take a look at this letter." George handed Jack a second letter.

Jack read the letter, and rather than skimming it as he did the first letter, he found himself reading slowly and diligently.

"This second letter is nothing like the first. I feel as though I was a fly on the wall in the meeting. I understand what the critical business issue is and why the company has that issue. It is quite detailed in that respect. Two-thirds of the letter documents the conversation from the prospects point of view. It also is devoid of the gratuitous remarks that made up the bulk of the first letter. Finally, there are a few next steps that seem clear and unambiguous. I've never seen a letter quite like this."

George leaned forward in his chair and looked straight at Jack. "I want my salespeople to be great detectives. I want them to find out what kinds of issues and challenges our prospects have and, very importantly, why they are having those issues. Only then can we begin to explore ways to solve them. And the only way we will get that kind of information is twofold:

"First, we must ask questions, not give presentations. By company decree, no salesperson in our company is allowed to bring more than a pad of paper and pens to first calls with prospects—no laptops, no collateral.

"Second, considering the behavioral map you learned about yesterday, most prospects will only reveal a great depth of information while they are in phase one of the buying process and to vendors whom they deem worthy. If the prospect is unwilling or unable to provide the needed information, we quickly begin to suspect there may be a problem with the opportunity. To confirm either case, we require all first calls to be followed by a sales follow-up letter summarizing all the important information that was discussed during the call."

"How did you come up with this methodology?" Jack asked.

"After realizing that buyer preferences are set early in the sales cycle, we looked for a way to confirm that in our sales process. We took a look at many sales methodologies that focused on both buyer behavior and good selling techniques. We wanted the process to align with what we know about the three phases of buying. And we wanted the approach to be auditable and

Sin 3—Lacking a Repeatable, Auditable Sales Process

not based on salespeople's opinions. We determined that there are several critical checkpoints in the buying phases that we can test. They all have to do with establishing and confirming buyer commitment. Ironically, although severely flawed, that was the implied goal of the old 'close early, close often approach.'

"The significant difference is that this approach is not manipulative because we, that is, our salespeople, support staff, and management really do need to understand buyer needs first. By requiring salespeople to document sales calls following a structured format, we can consistently validate buyer intent *and* our correct understanding of buyer need."

Jack responded, "I noticed that the letter does not mention anything about your value proposition."

"Good observation. Through experience, we have found that the best follow-up correspondences are those that are completely devoid of the salesperson's opinion. So even statements such as 'I enjoyed meeting you,' while polite, may sound gratuitous or insincere despite our best intentions. It really doesn't add anything to the purpose of the discussion. So, selling is not allowed. Prospects conclude early in the sales cycle if salespeople are trustworthy or not. Ironically, the less we sell in the traditional ways, the better we do. I would go so far as to say that if we are spending a lot of time with a buyer and we are fairly sure they are in phase one, our win rate is over 80 percent."

"You mentioned that the stages are auditable. How does that work?"

George answered, "As you can see from the letter, there is quite a bit of detail about what was discussed, including the critical business issues that the prospect has. The only way this letter can be produced is if the prospect shared this information and the salesperson listened and took good notes. That is the correct buyer and seller behavior in phase one. If I want to know what is going on in the account, I simply ask for the correspondence between the prospect and our company. There is a specific type of correspondence at each stage in the buying cycle. Based on what I read, I can determine what stage the buyer is in and how we are doing."

Jack thought about that for a few minutes. Acme already had a sales process, but now he could see a significant difference between the approach that George just described and theirs. The Acme process was based on the actions the salespeople took, such as making presenta-

Sin 3—Lacking a Repeatable, Auditable Sales Process

tions and giving demos. The reaction of the customer at each of those stages was graded by the salesperson and the sales manager. It was based on their instincts as to whether the opportunity was hot or not. It wasn't very objective. That was the problem. Salespeople believe what they want to believe and have great hope that things will swing in their favor. That was the reason for the consistently overly optimistic forecast.

"Jack, does this make sense?"

"Yes George. Everyone in your company is following this methodology?"

"Yes, for the most part they do. It does take some practice to master all the elements and to understand how it works. As a salesperson has success with each element of the process, he or she becomes more and more convinced of its validity. This was a fundamental behavior change for most of our salespeople, who were taught many of the old-style manipulative tactics or simply had no idea that sales could be managed as a process."

George continued, "I must admit, my eyes were opened. Think about it. We have GAAP accounting procedures, and since we are public, we have to follow Sarbanes-

Oxley and other financial rules and procedures. In our development labs, we have source code control procedures and engineering guidelines that everyone must follow. Why don't companies put as much effort into developing best practices for the revenue machine as they do everything else?"

"Makes sense," replied Jack. "I thought I knew all about sales and the sales process, and I thought we just didn't have the right combination of people, management, and sales pitch. My eyes have been opened too. How did you manage to get all this into place? How did you get started?"

"I'll give you the name of the people that helped us. I should let you know that their approach is not just about teaching salespeople to sell better. To be successful, you, Jack, have to make an equal commitment to holding the rest of management accountable for the process."

Jack had already made a commitment to improving the results of his company, and it was increasingly evident that the board of directors was willing to make that same commitment. Now his job was to get the management team on board with this approach.

Sin 3—Lacking a Repeatable, Auditable Sales Process

The two had spent the better part of four hours going over the details of the sales process that George used in his company. George explained that beyond the benefit of improving their selling effectiveness, it also helped them be on the same page with prospects and customers. In their case, more than 70 percent of their business was repeat business with existing customers. However, the competitive landscape was such that they had to be vigilant at all times. George explained that the same processes and methodology that his company used for gaining new business was equally effective at building and expanding business with their existing customer base. The deadly sin was not having a repeatable, auditable sales process.

Jack asked why he had not heard about such a methodology before and why George had never made mention of its use previously.

"The answer is simple," George explained. "Our sales approach is a competitive weapon. The fact that all my competitors insist on telling their story with great fanfare, on creating lots of beautiful collateral, on making presentations, and on giving demos helps our cause. Instead, when we take the time and patience to really understand what our prospects and customers need and when we can clearly articulate those needs from their point of view, we win. Why would we want anyone else to find out?"

The last point really hit home for Jack.

SIX

Sin 4—
Relying on Technology to Forecast Revenue

ON THURSDAY MORNING, Jack Ressler finally made it to his office. He had spent the past three days meeting with board members learning about the deadly sins he had committed, and this day was no different. But today, Mark Jones was coming to Jack's office. As Jack made his way to his office, he could feel the eyes of employees and management alike as they tried to determine by Jack's expression and stride what was going on.

He was still processing all the information that he had received so far and the impact of the sins that he had committed. So far he knew about three CEO selling Sins:

1. Confusing marketing with selling
2. Failing to understand how buyers buy

FIVE DEADLY SINS

3. Lacking a repeatable, auditable sales process

After sitting at his desk, Jack stared at the yellow pad of paper on which he had written. If nothing else, it was accurate. He had made those errors. Perhaps he felt a little better that many other people had too. As George Purdum had pointed out the day before, there was a huge opportunity for companies that could use their approach to selling as a strategic weapon. George had argued that few companies really have any kind of structured sales process; therefore, anyone who did could easily distinguish themselves. With customers and prospects having greater difficulty differentiating between companies' products and services, Jack felt it was helpful knowing that there were other ways to compete beside price and product.

At 10 o'clock sharp, Jack's assistant interrupted his train of thought to announce that Mark Jones had arrived. Mark was the most recent addition to the board of directors, so he and Jack hadn't had a chance get to know each other. However, this was the fourth meeting that Harry had arranged, so by now Jack knew to expect the unexpected.

Mark Jones was a member of the private equity firm

Sin 4—Relying on Technology to Forecast Revenue

that led the financing for Acme and was the partner representative on the board. He was involved with more than a dozen companies, and according to Mark, no two were alike. Mark was a numbers guy and was usually asking about margin percentages, CAGR, and free cash flow analysis. In a pleasant way, Mark seemed a bit geeky but always had valuable comments and observations.

Mark bounded into the office and firmly shook Jack's hand. "Good morning, Jack. Good to see you!"

"Hi Mark, thanks for coming in. I really appreciate—"

"Not at all," Mark interrupted. "Glad to help." It seemed that Mark knew what Jack was going to say before he said it.

"I know I am supposed to discuss the fourth deadly sin with you, but I only have an hour. Hopefully, that will be enough time."

"What is the fourth sin," asked Jack.

"The fourth sin is relying on technology to forecast sales."

"Hm, I don't think I follow you," said Jack.

Mark replied, "At the board meeting you shared some screen shots of the dashboard that is generated by your sales management and tracking system. Can you bring that up on your computer?"

"Yes. Certainly."

Jack logged into the company system and brought up the executive dashboard that Mark wanted to see. On the screen were a set of charts that showed the total forecast of revenue with comparisons to budget and prior year. At the click of a mouse, Jack could select year-to-date, quarter-to-date, and month-to-date. There were also a few charts that indicated the number of new accounts, the number of prospect calls, the customer and prospect visits, and the number of proposals issued.

"Yes, that's it," said Mark as he stood behind Jack and watched. "Looks impressive."

"But ..." Jack began.

"It's not so much a question of what it shows, but rather what you are tracking," said Mark. "When I first saw this at the board meeting, I hoped that you would explain how this system was helping you. I got the dis-

Sin 4—Relying on Technology to Forecast Revenue

tinct impression that the fact you had a way to track sales using automation was the biggest benefit."

"It is," Jack protested. "It took a lot of effort to come up with a system that everyone said they would use. It took even more effort to finally get salespeople to put in the necessary information. Initially, they were not very happy about it."

"Why not?"

"First, we asked them to put in their entire prospect and contact information. Once that was complete, we implemented a sales process." Jack froze. He realized that they had put in a process designed by management, for management. It was nothing like the sales process that George and he discussed the day before. It was also not in alignment with the way people and companies buy.

"The sales process we have requires salespeople to record all their customer and prospect activities such as calls and visits," Jack explained. "We have separate notations for different stages: demonstrations, site visits, et cetera. As the stage of each opportunity changes, we ask our salespeople to update the system and assign a deal value and probability."

"How reliable is it?"

"I think we know the answer to that question. More importantly, based on what I've learned so far this week, I think I understand why," Jack said.

Mark sat silent as Jack continued.

"There are three problems," began Jack. "First, we are relying on the opinion of salespeople to estimate probabilities. Not only do we have people with widely different experiences and talent, they also have very different ways of managing the sales process. No two are alike, and a single salesperson rarely does things the same way twice. When pressed, they will usually say the situation is better than it really is. That makes the data we get wildly optimistic, exaggerated, inconsistent, and generally unreliable. To get to the bottom of each opportunity, our sales managers have to discuss each opportunity with the salespeople to try to validate the data. That takes a significant amount of time, while the salesperson essentially relives each sales call with his or her manager.

"Our sales managers could each spend up to ten hours a week in these types of discussions. All that time is being used to analyze where we are. Not only is the accu-

Sin 4—Relying on Technology to Forecast Revenue

racy questionable, the time is not being spent working on tactics and strategies about where we need to go."

Jack paused to look at Mark. Jack was on a roll as all the ideas and concepts of the past several days were converging in his head. He was getting excited about where the conversation was going.

"The next problem with the way we have approached using our technology is that we are tracking activity. I always thought that selling was about the numbers: the more calls we make, the more sales we generate."

Mark jumped in. "If your salespeople make a thousand bad calls, making two thousand bad calls isn't going to help much. Most companies miss this point."

Jack added, "We're tracking how many calls are made and how frequently. What we really want to do is track whether a prospect or customer has told us about a business issue that is urgent and important and is one that they must solve."

"Yes," Mark said. "You want to know what stage in the selling process they are in. How you find that out requires a completely different approach to customer interaction. It should also make sense that the way the tracking system is used and what kind of data is fed into it should change to match the sales process and not the other way around."

Jack realized that the last point echoed a comment that his CFO made months ago. Once the executive dashboard had gone live, Jack had felt much better about the sales forecasts and the prospects for growth in the business. His CFO didn't share the same enthusiasm, and Jack was never quite sure why. After all, if the pipeline started to decline they would have an early warning of a potential problem. He had felt a sense of comfort knowing that all the sales leads and follow-up activities were being tracked in the system.

His CFO had two concerns:

- the rule of numbers, and
- salespeople gaming the system.

If there were a large number of inputs from the sales organization, over time Sam could calculate the error rate of forecast to actual and build in a factoring percentage that would approximate the actual results. As long as there was a stable market, a constant production capacity of the sales, and no significant economic or competitive factor, he could estimate the revenue

Sin 4—Relying on Technology to Forecast Revenue

number. But that was never the case, so he always cut that number down further to try to anticipate unexpected events. In other words, the forecast was needlessly conservative because it was based on looking backwards at historical trends and not based on solid factual evidence for future results. As it was, even conservative projections were not enough to anticipate the drop-off in business that Acme had during the prior quarter.

Jack noticed the third problem when he looked more closely at specific opportunities that closed during the quarter. In more than just a few instances, there were deals that suddenly appeared on the revenue report that were not listed during the early part of the quarter. These so-called blue-birds, while welcomed, just served to highlight the lack of visibility management had on an opportunity by opportunity basis.

On that last point, Jack had a fairly good idea what had happened. In their zeal to improve the accuracy of the forecast, management had created an unintended consequence. They were putting lots of pressure on salespeople to close business and to be accurate with their forecasts. As a result, some salespeople were taking very conservative views toward opportunities until they had a contract in their hand. Once assured of the business, they would post the opportunity or rapidly upgrade its percentage probability.

"So you see," said Mark, "relying on technology to forecast only works when you have a well-defined sales process in place already. Doing it the other way around can lead to some very bad behavior. None of that helps you or your customers."

"And that is the fourth deadly sin," said Jack.

"That's it. You did most of the talking today, but by the sound of things, you seem to be on the right track. Is there anything else I can help you with?"

"Not right now. I have a lot of work ahead of me to get this fixed," replied Jack.

"Not really. When you are ready with a plan, all of us can help find you the resources you need to execute it." On his way out the door, Mark said, "Knowing what to do is the hard part. See you next week."

Jack went back to the desk where he kept the yellow pad and filled in one more line on the page.

4. Relying on technology to forecast revenue.

SEVEN

Sin 5—
Promoting Star Athletes to Head Coach

It was finally Friday. The weather was beautiful, and Jack was scheduled to meet with Avery Skillman to learn about the fifth deadly sin. Avery had asked Jack to meet her at the local high school at 4 p.m. It seemed an odd place to meet, but the idea of leaving a few minutes early sounded fine to Jack. His management team had peppered him for the better part of two days trying to uncover what was afoot. They all knew that the quarter results were not good since the announcement went out. What they didn't know was that the board had rallied behind Jack to help him address the five deadly sins CEOs make in sales.

Avery Skillman's company had fewer than two hundred people. Despite its small size, the company was well-known because it was a repeated winner of the local Best Small Company to Work For award. That achievement happened to have been picked up by a national entrepreneurial magazine that decided to feature Avery on one of their monthly covers. The subject of the article was leadership coaching. Since then, Avery had been inundated with speaking requests from all over the country. She hated to turn anyone down, but she still had to run her company. Nevertheless, the public relations value for her company was fantastic. As a matter of fact, Harry Green saw an article about Avery and her company and decided to ask her to join his board of directors.

Jack caught up to Avery in the stands of the school stadium. "Hi, Avery."

"Hi, Jack. Are your ready for some sports entertainment?"

"Sure, but I thought we were going to talk about my sins?"

"Oh, we'll get to that," laughed Avery. "I thought you might enjoy some high school soccer. My son is on the team."

"How is the team?"

Sin 5—Promoting Star Athletes to Head Coach

"Unfortunately, they usually lose. Half the team members play year round. The rest are fall season only participants. Except for a few teams in the state, that is fairly typical."

"I see. Then what's the difference between this team and the others?" asked Jack.

"That is the subject of our discussion today: coaching."

Jack looked out onto the field to see the players lining up to start the game. From outward appearances, he couldn't tell any difference between the teams. Except for the color of their uniforms, they looked the same. Once the game started, Jack confirmed what Avery had said.

It didn't take long for the opposing team to score several goals. Avery waited until the whistle blew for halftime to continue the conversation with Jack.

"What do you think?" asked Avery.

"Your son's team is working very hard, but they don't look very organized."

"Can you be more specific?"

"I guess I noticed the other team passed a lot more. It seemed that every time the home team got the ball, they would run with it. It usually didn't take long for two opposing players to converge and steal the ball away."

"Good catch," said Avery.

Jack asked, "Is this connected in some way to a deadly sin?"

"It's not as big a leap as you might expect. First, let me tell you that our team has had the same coach for four complete seasons and has never had better than a .300 season. You might also be surprised to learn that the head coach was a multi-sport All-American athlete, including soccer."

"So why are they having so much trouble?" Jack asked. "I would think that since the coach is so talented and knows the game that he could teach the kids."

"That is the deadly sin," Avery replied.

"What do you mean?"

"Just being a great athlete is not a proper qualification to coach. I am sure you have seen Michael Jordan play

Sin 5—Promoting Star Athletes to Head Coach

basketball. He was amazing. Did you also know that he had a great deal of difficulty, even frustration, when he tried to manage the Charlotte Bobcats?"

"Yes, I recall reading about that. Eventually he hired a general manager to run the team."

"The problem with great athletes is that they don't know what they are doing. I mean that literally. When really great athletes perform, they often rely on instinct to direct their innate talent. They don't think about all the steps and techniques while they are performing. As the sports company slogan says, they 'Just Do It.' Getting to that level of greatness required lots and lots of practice. However, depending on how they were trained and by whom, great athletes rarely have the time or inclination to break the moves down into discrete steps. They almost always practice the entire, integrated move or skill. In many cases, they can see a picture in their mind of what they want to do before they do it. The effort appears seamless and effortless. That is what distinguishes great athletes."

"I understand what you're saying. I've seen that before," Jack said.

"Yes," said Avery. "The worst thing that can happen is

assigning a star athlete to coach without proper training. The star athlete often starts with a self-analysis to determine what helped him or her achieve great performance. In almost every case, it comes down to motivation. Therefore, since it worked for them, motivation becomes the primary incentive to try to coax better performance from other players. Even if a player wants to do better, there is a natural limitation to actual ability.

"When motivation doesn't produce the desired results, the star athlete-turned-coach may become frustrated. Since motivation didn't work, they change tactics. For example, the coach may tell the team that they are not trying hard enough or that they don't have the desire or will to win. The fact is that they could have all the desire in the world to win, but if they lack the training and skills, it will never happen.

"After motivation fails, the next tactic the coach may use is fear. Penalties are introduced for a lack of performance. Those consequences are meant to spur the team on to better performance. But penalties usually result in further frustration by the team members. Not all athletes are equal. Some players respond to this approach, while others don't. That results in the coach segmenting athletes into favorites and nonfavorites. In team sports this is a recipe for failure.

Sin 5—Promoting Star Athletes to Head Coach

"The whole point is that the majority of athletes are not star athletes. Most of the team needs specific and detailed instructions about how they should perform a specific function on the team. Then they need to practice that skill over and over again until they are proficient. Once mastery of one skill is achieved, additional skills can be added.

"Where team sports are concerned, each member must also be taught how to function effectively with the other members so that the team can function as one. Trust is established as team members learn, through practice, to expect, and even anticipate, what other members will do. In this way, team members can substitute for their teammates in the middle of the game, and the team still keeps functioning as one unit."

Avery paused to take a breath and to let what she had just described sink in. After a moment, she continued.

"Our coach is a star athlete who has not recognized that the way his team performs on the field is a mirror image of they way he coaches them in practice. What he teaches in practice is what he knows worked for him. What worked for him is his individual, star athlete style of performance. As a result, he tends to reward individual performance and favors those athletes who are a little better than the others. The net result is that our team is consistently beaten by teams who are coached to perform as a team instead of coached based on individual performance. And, as I mentioned, the two primary levers he tries to use to improve the team performance in games is fear and motivation. It just doesn't work.

"What you saw in the first half was the manifestation of his coaching approach. They have less teamwork than the other team and few, if any, substitutions. He simply keeps the best players in. What you will see by the end of the game is that the best players are dog tired and burn-out sets in. As that happens, the team performance deteriorates further. In turn, they get frustrated with themselves and their teammates, and that will reinforce a breakdown of whatever team play they had."

Something was beginning to gnaw at Jack's brain as he listened to Avery's animated description of the soccer team's dilemma. He could tell she was passionate about the topic and that she had a very deep understanding of coaching best practices. He felt she really knew what she was talking about.

"Have you ever thought about having a discussion

Sin 5—Promoting Star Athletes to Head Coach

about this with the coach?" Jack asked. "I understand you were also an accomplished athlete, and you are recognized as a successful business person with a specialty in leadership coaching."

Avery smiled at Jack, realizing he had checked into her background.

"Another characteristic of star athletes is that they tend to have big egos and always like to be in control. Until a sense of humility sets in and they ask for help, any advice is considered unwelcome meddling. In their minds, their past accomplishments qualify them as experts in their field. Most don't realize that their performance skills do not qualify them for coaching. That is not to say that a star athlete can't learn to coach. Most don't realize they don't know how. In particular, they don't like to fail. As a result, they don't take advice very well. For that reason, I have never had a discussion with the coach about coaching practices."

"That's too bad. I bet he could benefit from your experience. He would probably be happier if he knew how to better help the boys."

"Someday, I hope."

As if lighting had struck him, Jack understood what Avery had been telling him. He had plucked a perfectly happy star salesman out of a competitor and put him in charge of the Acme sales organization. Bill Smith was a star athlete trying to coach, and he was struggling. What's more, Jack had made the decision to hire him without the proper coaching skills or training. Without that, he may have set him up to fail. Bill had been making many of the same mistakes that the soccer coach had been making. He used the same two levers to instill performance: motivation and fear. His method of teaching was to have salespeople shadow him on sales calls. They were instructed to watch and listen to what he did and then copy him. This correlated closely to the emphasis on individual athlete performance that Avery was describing.

Jack wasn't even sure that Bill knew what he was doing in front of prospects and customers. He just winged it. But he wasn't teaching it in a way that others could emulate. If they could do it on their own by observing Bill once, then almost by definition they would be star athletes.

Jack knew that most of the sales organization was not capable of that kind of osmosis. Instead, they would require someone to break down the steps of the sales

Sin 5—Promoting Star Athletes to Head Coach

process and then coach them as they mastered each of the skills. The other concern Jack had was that many of their sales situations required more than one person to be involved. He had seen in the past that his people didn't always work well together on prospect or customer calls. Everyone had an opinion of what should be said and done. The result was that they didn't look very professional or well-organized, and Jack was sure that their audience of potential clients picked up that fact.

Avery was studying Jack's face as he stared off into space. He was deep in thought.

"Jack, are you still there?"

Jack came back to the conversation. "That's it then; isn't it? The fifth deadly sin is that I promoted a star salesman to head coach or, in this case, vice president of sales?"

"Yes, you did. It's a little different because your vice president of sales works for you and could probably figure it out if you help him."

"What do I do now?" Jack asked both himself and Avery.

"Not all top sales performers are cut out to be managers. Managers have to administer, and that is one thing that many top performers are unwilling or unable to do. On the other hand, if your vice president of sales is both willing and able to learn what you have learned this week, then there is hope. That discussion will have to be between you and him, and I imagine it will take some soul-searching on both your parts to decide how to proceed.

"If you do decide that you want to implement a structured sales process and you feel that Bill is the one to lead the effort, I would be happy to work with him on the skills necessary to implement it. That is what coaching leadership is all about. I don't know how we expect great salespeople to become great coaches unless we train them. Only 10 percent of the top 10 percent of great salespeople are also naturally gifted coaches. That's only 1 percent of all salespeople. This doesn't mean the rest can't coach. It means that we have to do the same thing we do to train salespeople. We have to codify the steps that great coaches use and show them to others.

"I am confident that Bill wants to become a better coach. First, you and he will have to get your hands dirty with rebuilding the sales engine of the company. When you

Sin 5—Promoting Star Athletes to Head Coach

get that done, let me know and I'll help you with the leadership aspects of sales management."

"Will do," replied Jack.

The whistle sounded, starting the second half, and the game began again. It wasn't much different than the first half, except a few players were moved around to new positions. That didn't seem to have much effect on the outcome as the opponents racked up a few more goals and the home team ran out of steam. The more Jack thought about his sales organization and their activities and results this year, the more parallels he saw between the field of athletics and the business world.

It had been a mentally exhausting week. Jack had met with five different board members to discuss what turned out to be very common business mistakes. Harry Green and the board called them sins, but Jack had not committed them consciously. He didn't know that he had followed the same flawed logic that many others had.

On Monday morning, he would reconvene the board to discuss his plans to fix the problem.

FIVE DEADLY SINS

His yellow pad was sitting on the front seat of his car. He could now complete the list of CEO selling sins:

1. Confusing marketing with selling
2. Failing to understand how buyers buy
3. Lacking a repeatable, auditable sales process
4. Relying on technology to forecast revenue
5. Promoting star athletes to head coach

EIGHT

A New Direction

ALL WEEKEND, JACK worked on a plan to address each of the deadly selling sins that he learned from the board members during the previous week. He made several plans before he came up with one he liked. He was surprised at how intertwined each sin was with the others.

Like many CEOs, his perspective on selling was simply to hire the best salespeople and tell them to sell. Of course, as he now realized, what makes a good salesperson and what makes a good sales manager are not the same. Furthermore, what he thought were good selling skills, such as the ability to make great presentations, were not the same skills needed to diagnose customer business issues with the goal of becoming a trusted advisor. In other words, deciding that someone is a good salesperson because he or she sounds and acts like a salesperson may be exactly the wrong conclusion.

Next, he realized that problems started when he did not work with Bill Smith to develop his managerial talents and to help him understand his selling instincts and how to break those down into discrete selling skills he could teach. Jack also realized that he had abdicated the design and development of the entire revenue generation machine to Bill. He erroneously figured that if Bill knew how to sell, he also knew how to implement the right sales process and how to build and manage a sales organization.

After that ball started rolling, he and Bill both agreed that installing sales tracking software would help them manage the forecast as well as manage what they thought was a sales process. That assumption led to further problems. They thought that having the raw data about number of leads, sales calls, and presentations would allow them greater control and visibility into the pipeline and revenue forecast. It was painfully clear from the quarterly results that the company did not have much idea what was going on. At that point, Jack felt embarrassed about having made his sales dashboard the highlight of a previous board meeting. The board members must have known, or at least suspected, something was wrong.

Jack now knew that without a repeatable and audit-

A New Direction

able sales approach, it was impossible to use any technology to manage sales or forecast results accurately. The so-called sales process they did have had very little correlation to the way buyers buy goods and services. Without understanding buyer behavior, how in the world could they improve the customer experience with Acme? The answer was, they couldn't.

Lastly, because he didn't understand any of this before, Jack's primary means to get the message out to convince buyers to buy from his company was going out and telling them. Telling versus asking was not working. Now Jack knew why. Certainly, his competitors were doing the same thing: making speeches and giving demos. This approach had the double impact of annoying prospects and preventing any valuable feedback and input from prospects and customers.

The first observable symptom of the five deadly selling sins was how the CEO and other senior executives conduct themselves with prospects and customers. All the rest of the issues were a matter of not taking the same approach with sales as the company did with other business disciplines, such as accounting and engineering. They needed a sales process.

The collection of books that Jack received from the

board members helped him synthesize these ideas. While he clearly understood what the company needed to do, he was certain that he didn't have inside the company all the expertise he would need to execute those changes. From prior experience, he knew that to make the behavioral changes necessary to properly align with customers, they would need outside help. Jack welcomed the recommendations and resources the board had already offered.

With notes in hand, Jack strode down the same hallway he had ten days before when he was dreading the outcome. Today, his confidence was soaring. He walked into the meeting room and greeted each board member with a strong handshake. His management team was there, too. Jack wanted everyone to hear what he expected to be the best meeting of his life.

With the laptop screen ready to go, the projector lights on, and the screen pulled down, Jack placed his notes on the table and looked around the room. Then very deliberately, he closed the notebook, turned off the projector, and flicked the switch to raise the screen.

"Let's talk."

APPENDIX

Jack's Meeting Notes

Notes:

1. The CEO sets the example; don't make presentations, have conversations.
2. Learn and understand how buyers buy.
3. Follow a sales process that is repeatable and auditable and that is consistent with buyer behavior.
4. Don't use sales tracking software to solve a selling problem. Track progress, not activity.
5. Promote great coaches. Teach great athletes how to coach.

An epilogue is available at:
www.FiveDeadlyCEOSins.com

References

Bosworth, Michael T. (1995). *Solution Selling*. New York: Irwin.

Bosworth, Michael T. and Holland, John R. (2004). *Customer-Centric Selling*. New York: McGraw-Hill.

Cranston, Mike. (2008). *Michael Jordan hires nomadic Larry Brown*. Available: www.usatoday.com/sports/topstories/2008-04-29.html. Last accessed August 2008.

Lewis, James B. (2007). *How to Hire a Contractor*. Available: http://www.princetonsalespartners.com/Howtohireacontractor.html. Last accessed October 2008.

Lewis, James B. (2007). *When do Sales Cycles really Begin?* Available: http://www.princetonsalespartners.com/Articles/WhenDoesaSalesCycleBegin.html. Last accessed November 2008.

Moore, Geoffrey A. (1991). *Crossing the Chasm*. New York: Harper Business.

Rackham, Neil (1988). *SPIN Selling*. New York: McGraw-Hill.

About the Author

JIM LEWIS IS the founder and CEO of Princeton Sales Partners, LLC, an executive management coaching and consulting firm to CEOs on the best practices of selling and sales management, located in Princeton, New Jersey. His sales process of choice is CustomerCentric Selling®.

His first sale was an Apple II computer to an Innovator. As instructed, his selling approach was to demonstrate the product and then watch to see if the buyer's eyes twinkled. Since then, Jim has learned how to correct the five deadly selling sins. For over twenty-five years, Jim has held numerous senior executive positions around the world and conducted business in forty countries.

Prior to founding Princeton Sales Partners, Jim was the CEO of Berlitz GlobalNET, a global services company with more than twenty thousand employees and contractors in eighteen countries. Prior to that, he was president of Globalink, a public AMEX technology company. Jim has initiated and been involved in more than fourteen acquisition events.

He is a certified instrument-rated pilot and a member of Angel Flight, for which he flies financially needy medical patients to healthcare facilities across America. Jim is also a certified Homeland Security Pilot First Responder.

More details are available at
www.PrincetonSalesPartners.com/AboutUs.html

Jim can be reached at:
Princeton Sales Partners LLC
66 Witherspoon, Ste 381 Princeton, NJ 08558
609-333-9785 direct 609-462-9924 mobile
JimLewis@PrincetonSalesPartners.com
www.PrincetonSalesPartners.com

Printed in the United States
209219BV00006B/13-69/P